GO FACTS SEASONS
Winter

A & C BLACK · LONDON

Winter

© Blake Publishing 2003
Additional material © A & C Black Publishers Ltd 2005

First published 2003 in Australia by Blake Education Pty Ltd

This edition published 2005 in the United Kingdom by
A & C Black Publishers Ltd, 37 Soho Square, London W1D 3QZ
www.acblack.com

ISBN-10: 0-7136-7282-X
ISBN-13: 978-0-7136-7282-4

A CIP record for this book is available from the British Library.

Written by Katy Pike
Design and layout by The Modern Art Production Group
Photos by John Foxx, Photodisc, Corel, Brand X, Corbis, Digital Stock,
Rubberball, Comstock, Stockbyte, Eyewire and Artville.

UK series consultant: Julie Garnett

Printed in China by WKT Company Ltd.

A & C Black uses paper produced with elemental chlorine-free pulp,
harvested from managed sustainable forests.

Contents

4 Signs of Winter

6 Plants in Winter

8 In the Garden

10 Winter Food

12 People in Winter

14 Animals in Winter

Signs of Winter

As autumn turns to winter, what changes can you see and feel?

Winter is the coldest season. The sun rises later and sets earlier. The days are shorter. Winter clothes need to be thick and warm.

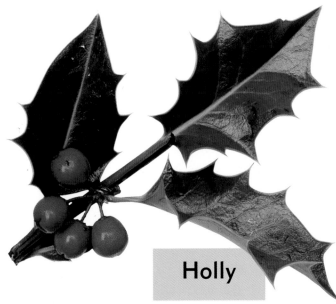

Holly

Sometimes it gets very cold. It may snow. Water may **freeze** on ponds, lakes and rivers.

A cold and frosty
winter morning.

GO FACT!

SHORTEST!
The shortest day of the
year is called the winter
solstice, on December
21st or 22nd.

Plants in Winter

Plants grow very little or not at all.

Deciduous trees have lost their leaves. The branches are bare.

Not all trees lose their leaves. Pine trees are green all year round. They are **evergreen** trees.

Some plants look like they are dead, but underground the roots and bulbs are still alive. The plants will grow again in spring.

Bare branch

Deciduous trees have bare branches in winter.

These trees will grow new leaves in spring.

Pine needles can live even after being frozen.

In the Garden

Most plants have stopped growing.

Gardens may look empty in winter. Vegetables have been harvested and flowers picked. Some garden plants die in winter. Others stop growing until the next spring. They are **dormant**.

In warmer countries, some vegetables, like broccoli and onions, grow slowly in winter.

Gardening tools

These lily bulbs will not grow until spring.

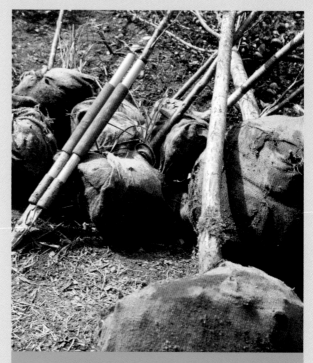

Trees can be planted in winter.

Pruning, or trimming, plants can be done during winter.

In winter some plants can be grown indoors. 9

Winter Food

Eating hot food makes people feel warmer.

In winter, people enjoy eating hot foods, such as soups and stews. Hot porridge is a healthy winter breakfast. Cocoa makes a warm winter drink.

Fruit preserves

Some people enjoy **preserves** in winter. In summer, fruits such as peaches and berries can be made into jams or canned to eat all year round.

Toast with jam

10

What is your favourite kind of soup?

Stews are usually cooked for a long time.

A hot drink tastes good on a snowy day.

People in Winter

People wear warm clothes because of the cold weather.

People wear more clothes in winter. Jumpers, heavy coats, scarves and gloves help keep us warm.

There are many winter sports. Some people like playing football or hockey. Other people like skiing down snow-covered mountains.

Winter clothes

You need waterproof gloves when you make a snowman.

Children carry a sledge out to the hills.

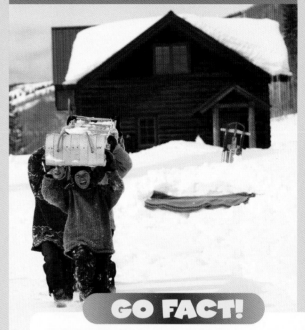

GO FACT!

DID YOU KNOW?

A Norwegian skier, Bjorn Dählie, has won more Winter Olympic medals than any other person. He has 12.

Being active keeps us warm when playing outside in winter.

Animals in Winter

Many animals spend more time sleeping in winter.

Border collie

Some animals **hibernate** or sleep through the winter. There are fewer plants and insects for them to eat.

Other animals like sheep, horses and dogs grow thicker coats. Some animals such as squirrels eat food they hid during summer and autumn.

Sheep and lamb

LONGEST!
The Siberian birch mouse hibernates for 8–9 months every year.

Cows grow thicker coats in winter.

Some horses wear turnout rugs in winter.

15

❄ Glossary

deciduous losing leaves in autumn

dormant not growing for a while; resting

evergreen having living, green leaves for the whole year

freeze change into ice

hibernate spend the winter sleeping or resting

preserves fruit cooked with sugar and kept in jars or cans

winter the coldest part of the year

❄ Index

clothes 4, 12

dogs 14

fruits 10

sheep 14

snow 4, 12

sports 12

sun 4

trees 6

vegetables 8

water 4